Caring for Fortunes

Logan Evans

Copyright Page

Index

The True Meaning of Wealth

The true meaning of wealth is not always the number of zeros in your bank account or the properties you own. While money can buy you many things, it does not necessarily guarantee you peace of mind, happiness or purpose in life. Being rich involves much more than accumulating assets; it is understanding how those assets impact your life and the lives of others. Without understanding this, wealth can become a burden rather than a blessing.

When you reach the point of being a millionaire, you realize that having money is just a tool. It is a means to achieve goals, not the goal itself. If you ever thought that reaching a certain amount of money would solve all your problems, you may have experienced a different reality. Money can eliminate material worries, such as paying off debts or covering basic needs, but it doesn't always solve internal problems, such as stress, loneliness, or lack of purpose. In fact, it can sometimes aggravate these problems if you are not clear about what you truly value in life.

Real wealth is about finding balance. It's not about living in fear of losing what you have, or spending it recklessly. It's about learning to enjoy your money without it becoming your only source of happiness. Many people fall into the trap of thinking that now that they're rich, they have to live surrounded by luxury to prove it. However, what really matters is not what others think of you, but how you feel about yourself and the decisions you make.

Another key aspect of the true meaning of wealth is time. Once money is no longer an issue, you begin to realize that time is your most valuable resource. You can buy a lot of things, but you can't buy more time. That's why taking care of your physical and mental health becomes essential. If you spend your days worrying about protecting every penny, you deprive yourself of the joy of living in the present. If you work tirelessly to multiply what you already have, without rest or time to enjoy it, then money loses its purpose.

It's also important to talk about relationships. Often times, wealth can affect how people relate to you. Some may admire you for what you have, while others may approach you with insincere intentions. That's why it's vital to surround yourself with people who value you for who you are, not your bank account. Authentic relationships are part of what truly enriches your life.

Finally, one of the greatest satisfactions that wealth can offer is the ability to help others. Philanthropy, whether on a large scale or simply helping those around you, gives a deeper purpose to your fortune. Knowing that you can make a difference in someone else's life creates a sense of gratitude and fulfillment that no purchase can match.

In short, the true meaning of wealth is understanding that it is not just about having, but about being. Being a balanced person, being generous, being authentic, and being aware that money is just a tool to build a life worth living. Money is important, but it will never be more valuable than the time, relationships, and positive impact you can leave on the world.

Protecting your Assets

Safeguarding your wealth is a crucial step once you've achieved financial success. No matter how much money you have, if you don't take steps to protect it, it will always be at risk. There are many threats that can jeopardize your wealth: lawsuits, economic downturns, fraud, and even planning mistakes. That's why it's essential to create a strong shield to ensure that what you've worked hard to build remains safe and well managed.

The first step to protecting your assets is to understand that you can't do it alone. Even if you have basic financial knowledge, you need a team of experts to help you cover all aspects of asset protection. These include specialized lawyers, trusted accountants, and financial managers. It's not just about delegating, but about making sure you're working with highly skilled people who have your best interests in mind. Hiring a bad advisor or failing to oversee the work of your team can be just as dangerous as doing nothing.

One of the most effective strategies for protecting your assets is the use of trusts. A trust is a legal tool that allows you to transfer your assets to an entity that will manage them for the benefit of you or your heirs. By doing so, these assets are protected from risks such as lawsuits or excessive taxes. In addition, trusts allow you to establish clear rules about how and when your assets can be used, making them an excellent choice for estate planning.

Another way to protect your wealth is to diversify it. Many people make the mistake of concentrating all their wealth in one place, such as real estate or company stocks. This can be very risky, because if something goes wrong in that sector, you can lose a large part of your fortune. Diversifying means spreading your investments across different areas, such as property, stock markets, index funds, precious metals, and even cryptocurrencies. The key is not to rely too much on a single source and to know the risks of each investment.

Using insurance is another critical component. Insurance is not an unnecessary expense; it is a safety net that protects you from unforeseen events. If you own property, make sure it is covered against natural disasters and accidents. If you own a business, consider liability insurance to back you up against potential lawsuits. It is also important to have life insurance to ensure that your loved ones will be protected if something happens to you. Although paying premiums may seem like a hassle, the peace of mind that these insurance policies provide is priceless.

Legal protection is another essential aspect. We live in a world where legal claims can arise at any time, sometimes even unjustifiably. Having a good lawyer review contracts, agreements and any important documents before you sign them can save you from costly problems. It is also advisable to separate your personal assets from your business assets, using structures such as partnerships or corporations to limit your liability.

One topic that is often overlooked is cybersecurity. In the digital age, your assets aren't just physical; they're online, too. From your bank accounts to your investments, all of your financial information can be vulnerable to attacks if you don't take proper measures. Use strong passwords, enable two-factor authentication, and keep your security systems up to date. Investing in a good cybersecurity advisor is just as important as any other aspect of asset protection.

Finally, it's important to regularly review your protection strategy. What works today may not be enough in a few years. Laws change, personal circumstances evolve, and threats can vary, too. Having regular reviews with your trusted team will allow you to adjust your plan and ensure it remains effective.

Protecting your wealth doesn't mean living in fear, but rather acting with caution and strategy. You've worked hard to build your fortune, and now it's your responsibility to protect it. Every step you take to protect your assets is a step toward peace of mind and security for yourself and your loved ones. The goal is not just to maintain your wealth, but to ensure that it will serve you well in living a full life and leaving a lasting legacy.

Smart Diversification

Smart diversification is one of the most important principles for protecting and growing your wealth. It's about not putting all your money in one place, because any investment, no matter how safe it may seem, always carries risks. By diversifying, you reduce the possibility of big losses and increase your chances of success in different areas. It's like building a boat with multiple compartments; if one takes on water, the rest can keep you afloat.

The most common mistake people who have accumulated wealth make is thinking that their main investment will always be safe. It might be a family business, a property, or stock in a company that has been doing well for years. But the market is constantly changing, and relying on just one source of income or one type of asset can be dangerous. Smart diversification allows you to spread those risks so that you don't have to worry if something unexpected happens in one sector or industry.

A good place to start is by identifying the main investment categories. These include real estate, stocks, bonds, index funds, precious metals, and now cryptocurrencies. Each of these options has different characteristics and plays a unique role in your portfolio. For example, real estate is known for being stable over the long term and generating passive income, while stocks can offer high returns over shorter periods, but with greater volatility. Precious metals, such as gold, are often safe havens in times of economic uncertainty.

A smart strategy is to allocate a portion of your wealth to each category based on your goals and risk tolerance. If you're looking for stability, you might invest more in real estate and bonds, which tend to be less volatile. If you're willing to take on more risk for higher returns, you might allocate a portion to high-growth stocks or cryptocurrencies. The key is to maintain a balance that fits your personal situation and to regularly review your investments to make adjustments as needed.

Within each category, it's also important to diversify. For example, if you're investing in real estate, don't put all your money into one country or property type. You might consider residential, commercial, or land properties in different markets. The same goes for stocks; instead of buying shares in just one company, invest in a diversified fund that includes companies from different sectors and regions. This protects you if a specific market faces problems.

Geographic diversification is also crucial. Financial markets and economies do not operate in isolation, but they do react differently to global events. Investing in different countries and currencies can protect your assets against changes in local policies, economic crises or currency fluctuations. However, it is important to study the tax and legal regulations of each region before investing.

A key part of smart diversification is knowing your limits. It's not about investing in everything just for the sake of it. You need to do your research and understand what you're putting your money into. If an investment option seems too complicated, consider working with a financial advisor who can help you make informed decisions. Remember that knowledge is one of your best allies in avoiding costly mistakes.

In addition to diversifying your financial assets, don't forget about investing in yourself. Education, continued learning, and skill development can be one of the surest ways to increase your wealth in the long run. If you stay up to date and understand market trends, you'll be in a better position to identify opportunities and avoid risks.

Finally, it's important not to let your emotions get the better of you. Sometimes fear or greed can influence your investment decisions, leading you to focus too much on an opportunity that seems "safe" or promising. Smart diversification isn't about chasing the latest fad, but about building a solid foundation that can weather any financial storm.

In conclusion, smart diversification is like building a garden full of different plants. Some bloom quickly, others take longer, but together they create a resilient and balanced ecosystem. By strategically spreading your investments, you protect your wealth, ensure a steady stream of income, and create a solid foundation for the future. The goal is not only to preserve your wealth, but also to give it the opportunity to grow safely and sustainably.

Global Financial Immunity

Global financial immunity is a concept that addresses how to protect your wealth in an interconnected world filled with uncertainty. No matter how much money you have accumulated, if you do not diversify and protect your assets globally, you are leaving your wealth vulnerable to risks such as local economic crises, currency fluctuations, regulatory changes, and geopolitical conflicts. This approach involves thinking beyond your home country and building a strategy that can withstand any eventuality, no matter where it occurs.

The first step to achieving global financial immunity is to understand that no economy is completely stable. Even the strongest countries can face recessions, banking crises, or political problems. That's why it's essential to diversify your investments across different jurisdictions. This includes opening bank accounts abroad, investing in international real estate, and having a portion of your portfolio in other countries' financial markets. By doing so, you reduce the impact of any problems that may arise in a single region.

A key tool to protect your assets globally is to open bank accounts in multiple currencies. Relying solely on one currency, even if it is strong like the US dollar, can be risky. Fluctuations in the exchange rate can erode your purchasing power or even cause you to lose money. By holding funds in different currencies, such as euros, Swiss francs or Japanese yen, you can balance these risks and ensure that you will always have access to liquid resources should the need arise.

International real estate investing is another effective strategy. Owning properties in different countries not only provides you with diversification, but can also be a source of passive income. For example, you could invest in a house in a tourist destination that generates rental income, or an apartment in a city with a growing economy. It is important to research each country's real estate market thoroughly and be aware of local laws before making decisions, as each jurisdiction has specific regulations for foreign investors.

Precious metals, such as gold and silver, are another essential component of a global financial immunity strategy. These assets have been considered a safe haven for centuries and have the advantage of being accepted and valued worldwide. Plus, you can store your precious metals in different countries, which adds another layer of protection. However, make sure to choose countries with political stability and strong legal systems to store these assets.

Offshore accounts are an option that many millionaires consider to protect their wealth. Not only do these accounts give you access to different financial markets, but they can also offer tax advantages depending on the jurisdiction. However, it is crucial to comply with all tax laws in your home country and declare these assets if necessary. It is not about evading taxes, but rather about optimizing your financial situation in a legal and transparent manner.

Global mutual funds are a practical way to diversify your assets globally without the need to manage them yourself. These funds are designed to invest in different regions, industries and asset types, allowing you to benefit from growth in overseas markets. In addition, they are usually managed by experts who have a deep understanding of international markets, which reduces the risk associated with direct investment abroad.

Another important aspect is access to residency or citizenship in other countries. Having an additional passport or a residence permit in a stable jurisdiction can be a significant advantage in the event of a crisis. Many countries offer investment programs that allow you to obtain residency or even citizenship in exchange for a significant investment in their economy, whether in real estate, business, or government bonds.

Cybersecurity is an increasingly important component of global financial immunity. With the digitalization of assets and the growing reliance on online platforms, protecting your financial data is more critical than ever. Use advanced authentication systems, keep your devices up to date, and consider hiring digital security services to ensure your information and assets are safe from cyberattacks.

Finally, continuing education is a must. The financial world changes rapidly, and what works today may not be enough tomorrow. Stay informed about global trends, new regulations, and investment opportunities in different countries. While working with experts is important, you also need to understand the fundamentals to make informed decisions and monitor your strategies.

In conclusion, global financial immunity is not just about protecting your wealth; it is a comprehensive approach to ensuring that your wealth is prepared for any situation. By diversifying your assets across different jurisdictions, currencies and sectors, you minimize risks and maximize opportunities. This approach not only gives you security, but also peace of mind, knowing that you have created a solid network that protects your future and that of the next generations.

Your Safety Net

Your financial safety net is like a cushion that protects you from unexpected events and allows you to maintain financial stability even in the most difficult times. It is the set of resources, strategies and decisions that you implement to ensure that, no matter what happens, you always have a backup. Without a solid safety net, even the largest fortunes can quickly evaporate. That is why building this network should be a priority if you want to protect your wealth in the long term.

The first element of a financial safety net is having an emergency fund. This fund is money set aside exclusively to deal with unexpected situations, such as an economic crisis, unforeseen medical expenses, or urgent repairs. Even if you have a high level of wealth, an emergency fund is essential because it provides you with immediate liquidity. The general recommendation is that this fund covers between six months and a year of your fixed expenses, and that it is deposited in an easily accessible account separate from your main investments.

Insurance is another crucial pillar of your safety net. No matter how careful you are, there are always risks you can't foresee. Life, health, property, and even liability insurance are key tools to protect your assets and your loved ones. For example, if you own valuable property, insure it against natural disasters, fire, or theft. If you have dependents, good life insurance can ensure their financial stability should something happen to you. In addition, liability insurance protects you in legal situations that could jeopardize your assets.

Diversifying your income streams also strengthens your safety net. Relying solely on one business or investment can be dangerous, as any changes in that sector could significantly impact your cash flow. If you have multiple sources of income, such as property rentals, stock dividends, royalties, or a side business, you reduce the impact of any setbacks in one area. Not only does this protect your wealth, it also creates a steady stream of cash that you can reinvest.

An often overlooked aspect is tax planning. Taxes can be one of the biggest threats to your wealth if you don't manage them properly. Work with tax experts to ensure you take advantage of all available legal deductions and structure your assets in a way that minimizes your tax liabilities. This isn't about avoiding taxes, but rather optimizing your finances so that you pay the right amount without compromising your wealth.

Creating a proper legal structure is also essential. This includes setting up trusts, companies, or family funds that protect your assets from lawsuits, legal issues, or family disputes. A trust, for example, can help you ensure that your assets are distributed according to your wishes and in a tax-efficient manner. Additionally, these structures can offer an extra layer of privacy and security from potential outside threats.

Your network of contacts is another crucial component of your safety net. Surround yourself with experts in different fields, such as financial advisors, lawyers, accountants, and business consultants. Not only can these people help you make informed decisions, but they also give you access to resources and knowledge that strengthen your financial position. Maintain constant communication with them and make sure they understand your long-term goals.

Also, never underestimate the value of continuing financial education. The world changes rapidly, and what works today may not be enough tomorrow. Stay up to date on new investment tools, changes in tax laws, and global economic trends. The more you know, the better equipped you will be to anticipate problems and adapt to changes.

Cybersecurity is another modern but indispensable element of a safety net. With digital threats on the rise, protecting your accounts and data is essential. Use strong passwords, two-factor authentication systems, and work with cybersecurity services to protect your digital assets. A breach in the security of your bank accounts or investments can have devastating consequences.

Finally, communication with your family and loved ones is part of your safety net. Make sure they understand your financial vision and that there is a clear plan in place in case of emergencies. This includes establishing a will, designating beneficiaries, and creating a succession plan for your businesses and properties. Open and transparent communication prevents misunderstandings and conflicts that could put your assets at risk.

In conclusion, your financial safety net is not a luxury, but a necessity. It is the foundation that supports your wealth and gives you the peace of mind that comes from knowing that you are prepared for any eventuality. Building this net takes time, effort, and planning, but the benefits are invaluable. With a solid safety net, you not only protect what you have achieved, but you also ensure a stable future for yourself and the generations to come.

Creating a Trustworthy Team

Building a trusted team is one of the most important steps to protecting and growing your wealth. No matter how smart and skilled you are, you can't do everything on your own. Building and maintaining wealth requires the help of experts in various areas who can advise you, perform specific tasks, and protect you from risks that aren't always visible. This team isn't just about hiring professionals, but about surrounding yourself with people you can fully trust, who share your vision, and who have a real commitment to your long-term goals.

The first step in building a trusted team is to identify the key areas in which you need support. These often include finance, legal matters, taxes, investments, business planning, and even personal or digital security. Each member of the team should be an expert in their field, with a proven track record of success and, most importantly, an impeccable reputation. For example, a good financial advisor can help you plan your investments, while an estate attorney can make sure your assets are legally protected.

One of the most important roles on your team is the financial advisor. This professional helps you structure your investment portfolio, assess risks, and maximize your returns. A good financial advisor not only seeks to multiply your money, but also to ensure that your decisions are sustainable and aligned with your goals. It is crucial that this advisor is completely transparent about his or her fees and has no conflicts of interest. Before hiring someone, do thorough research, ask for references, and make sure they understand your long-term goals.

The accountant is another key pillar. Handling taxes and making sure you comply with all tax regulations is vital to protecting your wealth. An experienced accountant will not only make sure your tax returns are correct, but will also find legal ways to optimize your taxes, helping you save money. In addition, they should be someone you can easily communicate with, as you will need to work closely on delicate and complex issues.

A trusted attorney is a must, especially when it comes to protecting your assets and ensuring that everything is in order from a legal standpoint. This professional can help you with creating trusts, drafting contracts, resolving legal disputes, and planning your estate. Make sure you choose someone with specific experience in estate and business law, as these are the fields that affect millionaires the most. Additionally, your attorney should have impeccable ethics and be committed to protecting your interests.

The investment manager is another key member of your team. This professional focuses exclusively on finding the best investment opportunities and actively managing your portfolio. An investment manager can help you diversify your wealth across different sectors and markets, reducing risks and maximizing your returns. Look for someone with a global vision, who understands market trends and has a strategic mindset. Also, make sure their incentives are aligned with yours – for example, that their compensation depends on the results you achieve.

Security, both physical and digital, is another aspect that you should not overlook when building your team. In an interconnected world, protecting your personal and financial data is just as important as protecting yourself and your family. Hire cybersecurity specialists who can ensure that your systems and devices are protected against potential attacks. On the other hand, if your lifestyle requires it, consider working with a physical security team that can protect your properties and ensure your peace of mind at all times.

The selection of each member of your team should be rigorous. Don't rush into hiring; spend time interviewing candidates, asking for references, and doing background checks. A bad choice can have serious consequences, from financial losses to legal conflicts. Also, make sure to set clear expectations from the beginning. Define specific roles, responsibilities, and goals for each team member. Open and transparent communication is key to keeping everyone working in the same direction.

Once you've assembled your team, it's crucial to build strong relationships based on mutual trust. This doesn't happen overnight; it takes time, honesty, and constant communication. Stay involved in important decisions and make sure all team members are aware of your long-term goals. Even though they may be the experts in their respective fields, you are the leader and should have the final say.

Finally, remember that a trusted team is not a static thing. Over time, your needs and goals may change, and some team members may no longer be a good fit for your circumstances. Regularly evaluate each member's performance and, if necessary, make changes. This doesn't mean you should distrust everyone, but be prepared to adapt to new situations and challenges.

In short, building a trusted team is not just a strategy, it is a necessity. Great fortunes are not built or protected alone; they require the support of skilled, committed people with impeccable ethics. By surrounding yourself with the best experts and establishing relationships based on trust, you will be building a solid foundation to protect and grow your wealth, guaranteeing not only your success, but also that of generations to come.

Avoiding the Mistakes of Overconfidence

Overconfidence is one of the most dangerous mistakes you can make when you have wealth. It's natural to feel confident after achieving financial success—after all, you've worked hard, made smart decisions, and overcome obstacles to get where you are. However, that same confidence can backfire if you start underestimating risks, ignoring advice, or assuming you'll always make the right decisions. Many great fortunes have been lost because those who managed them believed they were invincible. Avoiding this mistake requires an open mind, self-criticism, and a healthy dose of humility.

The first step to avoiding overconfidence is to recognize that past success does not guarantee future success. Markets, economic trends, and personal circumstances are constantly changing. An investment that was profitable five years ago may not be profitable today, and a strategy that worked in one specific market may fail in another. For example, if you made your fortune in real estate, you might fall into the trap of thinking that any property you buy will be a success. This mindset can lead you to take unnecessary risks, ignoring clear signs that the market is saturated or in decline.

Another aspect of overconfidence is believing that you know everything. While it's true that you probably have a lot of experience in your field, no one can be an expert in everything. When you start making important decisions without consulting experts or doing enough research, you set yourself up for costly mistakes. Imagine deciding to invest in cryptocurrency simply because you heard that someone else made millions. Without a deep understanding of the market, you could make impulsive decisions based on incomplete or erroneous information, which could result in huge losses.

Overconfidence can also lead you to underestimate risks. You may think that because you have faced and overcome challenges before, any future problems will be easy to handle. However, this type of thinking can leave you vulnerable. For example, you might not consider adequate insurance for your property or business because you trust that "nothing bad will happen to you." This is a serious mistake, as unexpected events can always happen, and not being prepared for them can put your assets at risk.

Financial arrogance is another way overconfidence can manifest itself. This occurs when you start making decisions based more on impressing others than on financial logic. Buying unnecessary assets, spending more than necessary, or entering into high-risk investments just to prove your success can all be signs of this problem. Not only is this type of behavior detrimental to your finances, but it can also affect your reputation and personal relationships.

To avoid overconfidence, it's essential to surround yourself with people who can offer you an objective perspective. A team of financial advisors, lawyers, and accountants will help you evaluate each decision from a professional, rather than emotional, point of view. Also, look for people in your inner circle who dare to question you and give you their honest opinion, even if it's not what you want to hear. These critical voices are essential to keep you grounded.

It's also important to develop the ability to question yourself. Before making any major financial decision, ask yourself whether you're acting on hard facts or simply on your intuition or past experience. Analyze the risks, research the options, and evaluate the potential consequences from all angles. This type of reflection will help you avoid impulsive decisions and allow you to take a more calculated and strategic approach.

Another key tip is to not let success cloud your judgment. Remember that wealth comes with responsibilities, and every decision you make can have a significant impact on your wealth, your future, and that of the people who depend on you. Keep a mindset of constant learning. Even if you are successful, there is always something new you can learn, whether it is about emerging markets, investment strategies, or financial management tools.

Diversification is also an effective way to protect yourself from overconfidence.

When you put all your resources into a single investment or sector, you're betting that your judgment will be perfect. But if something goes wrong, the losses can be devastating. Diversifying your investments and income streams reduces this risk and gives you greater security, even if you do make a mistake.

Finally, never forget that humility is a virtue in the financial world. Recognizing that you don't know everything, that you can make mistakes, and that there is always something to learn is a sign of strength, not weakness. Humility will allow you to listen to others, adapt to new circumstances, and, above all, protect your wealth from the dangers that sometimes come from your own mind.

In short, overconfidence can be a silent enemy that threatens your fortune if you don't take steps to control it. By keeping an open mind, surrounding yourself with experts, diversifying your decisions, and always remembering that wealth is not invulnerable, you will be better prepared to face challenges and preserve what you have built with so much effort. True financial success is not just about making money, but about keeping and growing it sustainably and consciously.

Investing in Private Businesses

Investing in private businesses can be one of the most interesting and profitable strategies to diversify and grow your wealth, but it is also one of the most complex and risky if not approached carefully. Unlike investments in public stocks, where you can analyze accessible data and follow market trends in real time, private businesses are often less transparent and more difficult to evaluate. However, with proper research and a well-thought-out strategy, they can offer exceptional returns and unique opportunities.

The first step in investing in private businesses is to clearly understand the type of company you want to be involved in. Not all private businesses are the same, and each sector has its own dynamics, risks, and opportunities. For example, investing in a small technology company can have enormous growth potential, but also a high level of uncertainty due to competition and the rapid evolution of the sector. On the other hand, a more traditional business, such as a restaurant or local services company, may offer more stable income but with less chance of multiplying your investment quickly. Knowing your risk tolerance and financial goals is essential to making informed decisions.

A key aspect when investing in private businesses is to assess the experience and skills of the management team. The quality of the people leading the business is often the most important factor in determining its success. Look for entrepreneurs who are not only passionate about what they do, but also have relevant experience, a clear vision, and a track record of overcoming challenges. If the founding team does not have a strong direction or understand their market, the company is likely to face problems, no matter how promising the idea seems.

Before investing, it's critical to conduct thorough due diligence. This means thoroughly analyzing all aspects of the business, including its finances, operations, target market, and future projections. Examine the financial statements to understand how the company generates revenue and how it uses its resources. Ask about its primary customers, operating costs, and any debt it may have. It's also helpful to research the market in which the business operates to assess whether there is sustainable demand for its products or services. Not only will this process help you identify potential risks, but it will also give you a better idea of the true value of the investment.

Once you have a good understanding of the business, it's important to structure the investment agreement in a way that protects your interests. This can include negotiating an ownership stake, voting rights, dividends, or even a position on the board of directors. While it's tempting to simply hand over money in exchange for a stake, a more active approach will allow you to have greater control and be more informed about the business's performance. Make sure you have clear, detailed contracts that spell out your rights and responsibilities, as well as the conditions for exiting the investment should things not go as you hoped.

Another aspect to consider is the time horizon of your investment. Unlike stocks or bonds, which can be sold relatively quickly, investments in private businesses are typically long-term. You should be prepared for your capital to be tied up for several years, as businesses need time to grow and generate significant returns. This long-term commitment can be a disadvantage for some, but it can also offer the opportunity to earn higher returns by supporting businesses in their early stages and participating in their future success.

Investing in private businesses also requires a careful approach to diversification. While it's exciting to bet on a company you believe in, putting all your money into one business is extremely risky. Even the most promising ideas can fail due to unforeseen circumstances, such as market changes, management issues, or new regulations. Therefore, it's advisable to spread your investment across several businesses and sectors to reduce the impact of potential losses.

Another important tip is not to invest solely based on your emotions. Sometimes, you may be drawn to an idea because it sounds innovative or because you personally like the product or service. However, emotions can cloud your judgment and cause you to overlook important issues. It is crucial to maintain an objective mindset and make decisions based on data, analysis, and a clear understanding of the business.

Networking also plays an essential role when investing in private businesses. Connecting with other investors, entrepreneurs, and industry experts can give you access to better opportunities and help you avoid common mistakes. Investment groups, angel investor networks, and business conferences are great places to learn from others and explore new possibilities. Plus, these connections can be invaluable when you need advice or support to manage your investments.

Finally, keep in mind that investing in private businesses is not just a matter of money, but also of time and energy. You will be more than just a shareholder; you will be a strategic partner who can influence the direction of the business. If you are willing to commit and work together with the team, you can add significant value to the company and increase your chances of success. However, if you prefer a more passive approach, it is important to set clear boundaries from the beginning and make sure that the business can function independently.

In short, investing in private businesses can be a rewarding and profitable experience, but it also requires preparation, patience, and careful management. By choosing businesses with potential, doing proper due diligence, diversifying your investments, and maintaining an objective mindset, you can maximize your chances of success while minimizing risks. With the right approach, you won't just be investing in a company, but in a vision that could become the next big thing.

Tax Planning for High Net Worths

High net worth tax planning is one of the most important strategies to protect and maximize your wealth. As your fortune grows, so does the complexity of your tax obligations. If you do not manage your taxes efficiently, you may end up paying more than necessary, which significantly reduces your net income and the value of your estate in the long term. Proper tax planning is not about evading taxes, which is illegal, but about ethically and strategically leveraging tax laws and regulations to your advantage.

The first step in tax planning is to understand the laws and regulations of the country where you reside, as well as those countries where you have investments or property. Each jurisdiction has its own tax rules, which may include taxes on income, capital gains, inheritance and gift taxes. Hiring an experienced high-net-worth tax advisor is essential to stay on top of your legal obligations and optimize your tax situation. This professional should be able to identify opportunities to legitimately reduce your taxes and ensure that you are in compliance with all regulations.

A common strategy in tax planning is to structure your investments and property in an efficient manner. This can include creating legal entities such as corporations, trusts, or foundations that allow you to manage your assets in a more flexible and tax-advantaged manner. For example, a well-designed trust can protect your assets from high estate taxes and ensure that your heirs receive your estate in an orderly manner. However, these structures must be created with a thorough understanding of local and international laws, as poor design can have negative consequences.

Geographic diversification also plays an important role in tax planning. Having assets and investments in different countries not only reduces financial risk, but can also offer tax advantages. Some countries have double taxation agreements, meaning you can avoid paying taxes on the same income in two different places. Others offer specific benefits to attract foreign investors, such as reduced tax rates or temporary tax breaks. However, managing an international portfolio requires constant analysis to comply with each country's regulations and take full advantage of their advantages.

One aspect that cannot be overlooked in high-net-worth tax planning is the handling of capital gains. These gains come from the sale of assets such as stocks, real estate, or businesses, and are often subject to specific taxes. An effective strategy to minimize this impact is to carefully plan the timing of sales. For example, if your profits are at a higher level during a particular year, you could postpone a sale until the following tax year, when you expect to have lower income. You can also use tax-loss strategies, offsetting gains with losses from other investments.

Tax planning also includes thinking ahead. This means considering how your current decisions will affect the transmission of your wealth to the next generations. Inheritance and gift taxes can be extremely high in some countries, but there are tools to reduce their impact. For example, making regular gifts during your lifetime to your heirs can help you distribute your wealth more efficiently and reduce the tax burden upon your death. Another option is to set up family trusts that protect your assets and reduce inheritance taxes.

Using life insurance can also be a powerful tool in tax planning. Some insurance policies not only provide financial protection for your loved ones, but can also offer significant tax advantages. For example, in certain cases, death benefits are tax-exempt, ensuring that your heirs receive a full sum without deductions. Additionally, insurance can be an effective way to pay estate taxes, as it provides immediate liquidity without the need to sell valuable assets.

Another crucial aspect of tax planning is the efficient management of passive income. Income from rents, dividends, royalties, or other sources may be subject to different tax rates depending on how it is structured. For example, some jurisdictions offer tax incentives for certain types of income, such as dividends from local businesses or income from investments in renewable energy. Working with a tax advisor will help you identify these opportunities and maximize your net income.

Philanthropy can also be an integral part of your tax strategy. Donations to charities not only have a positive impact on society, but can also significantly reduce your tax burden. In many countries, qualified donations are tax-deductible, meaning you can donate a portion of your income instead of paying it in taxes. Additionally, establishing your own charitable foundation can offer additional tax benefits and allows you to direct your resources toward causes you care about.

It's important to mention that tax planning is not a one-time activity. Tax laws change over time, and what works today may not be valid tomorrow. That's why it's essential to review and update your tax plan regularly, especially when you experience major changes in your financial situation or in the laws of your country. Maintaining constant communication with your tax advisor will help you be prepared for any changes and adjust your strategy accordingly.

In short, high net worth tax planning is an essential tool for protecting and growing your wealth. By understanding tax laws, structuring your assets efficiently, diversifying geographically, managing capital gains, and planning for the future, you can minimize your taxes and maximize your income. With the right support and a proactive approach, you can ensure that your fortune is well protected and that you take advantage of every available opportunity to optimize your tax situation. This will not only benefit you, but also future generations who will benefit from your planning.

Family Legacy and Financial Education

Family legacy is not only measured by the material goods you leave to your heirs, but also by the values, knowledge and principles you pass on. Financial education is one of the most valuable tools you can provide to your children and family members. It is not just about teaching them how to manage money, but about instilling in them a responsible and conscious mindset so that they can preserve and grow the family wealth in a sustainable manner.

A common mistake among high net worth families is to assume that wealth will solve all future problems. The reality is that without a solid foundation of financial education, money can become a source of conflict or even disappear within a generation. Studies show that many family fortunes are lost in the second or third generation due to a lack of planning and education. That's why taking the time to teach your heirs about finances is not only a good practice, but an investment in the stability and future of your family.

The first step to fostering financial literacy in your family is to create an environment of open dialogue about money. Talking about finances should not be a taboo subject. Explain to your children how you manage your income, expenses, and investments, and why you make certain financial decisions. Do it in a way that they can understand based on their age. For example, you can teach younger children basic concepts such as saving part of their allowance or understanding the value of work. As they get older, you can introduce more complex topics such as compound interest, investment diversification, and the importance of avoiding unnecessary debt.

It is essential to teach your children that wealth comes with responsibility. This includes not only taking care of material goods, but also using resources wisely and purposefully. An effective way to instill this value is to involve them in philanthropic activities from an early age. Allow them to participate in decisions about family donations, show them how their contributions can positively impact the lives of others, and explain to them why it is important to give back to society. This practice not only fosters empathy, but also helps them understand that wealth is not just for personal benefit.

Practice is key to consolidating financial knowledge. Provide your children with opportunities to handle money realistically. For example, you can give them a small sum to invest in a personal project or in the stock market under your supervision. This will allow them to learn firsthand about the risks, rewards, and responsibilities associated with money management. You can also use examples from everyday life, such as planning a family budget for a trip or comparing prices when purchasing something important.

Another crucial aspect of financial education is teaching them to differentiate between needs and wants. In a world where advertising and social media encourage overconsumption, it is easy to fall into the trap of spending on unnecessary things. Help your children develop a critical mindset when it comes to consumption. Teach them to evaluate whether a purchase is really worth it or whether that money could be used in a more productive way. This does not mean depriving them of enjoying their wealth, but rather guiding them towards a healthy balance between spending, saving and investing.

To build a strong family legacy, it's also essential to establish shared values and goals. Talk with your family about what wealth means to you and how you want it to be used. Some families develop a mission or vision that guides their financial and business decisions. This statement may include principles such as ethics, hard work, sustainability, or community engagement. Having a shared vision can bring family members together and minimize conflicts related to wealth.

Also, consider documenting your family's history and how the fortune was built. Sharing anecdotes about the effort, decisions and sacrifices that led to success can inspire future generations to value what they have and work to maintain it. You can even create a family book or video that chronicles these aspects and reinforces the sense of ownership and responsibility towards the heritage.

Don't forget that continuous learning is vital. Just as the financial world evolves, so should your family's knowledge. Encourage your heirs to read books, take courses, or participate in seminars on finance and investing. You can even invite experts to give family workshops to delve deeper into specific topics. Staying up to date will not only allow them to make better decisions, but will also boost their confidence in managing wealth.

Finally, remember that you are the most important role model for your family. Your actions speak louder than your words. If you manage your finances wisely, plan for the long term, and demonstrate generosity, your children are more likely to adopt those same habits. It's not about being perfect, but about being aware that your financial decisions are a direct example for them.

In short, family legacy and financial education go hand in hand. Leaving a fortune without teaching how to manage it is like giving a sports car without instructions on how to drive it. By providing your children and family members with the necessary tools to understand and manage money, you will not only be ensuring the preservation of your wealth, but also strengthening the family unit and preparing them to face the future with confidence and success.

Financial education is not a waste of time, it is an investment in future generations.

Strategic Philanthropy

Strategic philanthropy is much more than donating money to a good cause. It is a way to contribute to the good of the world with a planned, measured and effective approach. While generosity is always valuable, strategic philanthropy allows your resources to have a much greater impact. It is about aligning your personal values and goals with specific causes, designing a plan to support those causes and measuring the results of your contribution. This approach not only benefits the organizations and communities you help, but it also enriches your life knowing that you are making a real and lasting difference.

The first step in practicing strategic philanthropy is to identify the causes that are most meaningful to you. Reflect on the issues you care deeply about or the areas where you feel you can contribute with the greatest impact. Maybe you are passionate about education, the environment, health, social equality, or technological innovation. Define what your priorities are and how they align with your personal values. This process not only helps you focus your efforts, but it also gives a clearer purpose to your philanthropic actions.

Once you've identified the areas you want to support, it's important to do your research. Get to know the organizations and projects that work in those areas. Not all initiatives have the same level of effectiveness or transparency, so it's crucial to make sure your resources will be used responsibly and efficiently. Look for organizations with a proven track record of success, clear goals, and accountability practices. You can review their annual reports, talk to leaders of those organizations, or even visit the projects in person to see how they operate.

Another key aspect of strategic philanthropy is setting specific goals for your giving. Rather than simply giving away money, decide what you want to accomplish. For example, if you support education, you may want to fund scholarships for underprivileged students, build a school, or implement a teacher training program. These clear goals allow you to measure the impact of your efforts and motivate you to keep going when you see tangible results.

Long-term commitment is another essential component. Often, the problems that communities and organizations face are not solved with a one-time donation. Strategic philanthropy involves creating lasting relationships and supporting initiatives consistently over time. This doesn't mean you have to commit all your resources to a single cause, but you should consider the value of building a sustained relationship with the organizations you support. Your ongoing contribution can ensure that their projects are more sustainable and effective.

Not all of the resources you contribute have to be financial. Your knowledge, skills, and network can also be powerful tools in strategic philanthropy. If you have experience in business, finance, technology, or other areas, you can offer advice to the organizations you support. You can also connect those organizations with other donors or strategic allies. This multifaceted approach not only multiplies the impact of your contributions, but also strengthens organizations and allows them to operate more efficiently.

A key aspect of strategic philanthropy is measuring results. It's important to evaluate how your resources are being used and what impact they are having on the causes you support. Not only does this help you confirm that you are achieving your goals, but it also allows you to adjust your strategy if necessary. For example, if a project is not delivering the expected results, you may decide to redirect your resources toward a more effective initiative. Measuring impact also gives you the satisfaction of knowing that your efforts are creating real change.

Strategic philanthropy doesn't have to be a solitary endeavor. You can involve your family, friends, or even colleagues in the process. Not only does this strengthen your personal ties, but it also helps multiply the impact of your actions. For example, you can create a family giving fund where everyone participates in deciding which causes to support. Or you can organize events to raise fundraisers and awareness about issues you care about. Collaboration can also open up new perspectives and enrich your philanthropic approach.

Also, consider how your personal investments can align with your philanthropic goals. For example, you can invest in companies or projects that promote the same causes you support with your donations. This is known as impact investing, and it's a way to put your money to work to generate both financial and social benefits. By combining philanthropy with conscious investing, you can maximize the impact of your wealth and contribute to positive change on multiple fronts.

It's important to remember that strategic philanthropy isn't about getting recognition or praise. While it can be nice to receive thanks for your contributions, the main goal is to make a difference in the lives of others and in the world. Keep the focus on the impact, not the attention you might receive. This not only ensures that your actions are authentic, but it also sets an example for others who may want to follow in your footsteps.

Ultimately, strategic philanthropy not only benefits those who receive your help, it also transforms your life. By dedicating yourself to causes that truly matter, you experience a sense of purpose and connection that is hard to match. Knowing that you are using your resources to build a better world gives you deep satisfaction and a legacy that will last long beyond your lifetime. Being strategic in your generosity not only increases the impact of your wealth, it also enriches your spirit and leaves a positive mark on the world.

Adapting to Changes

Adapting to change is an essential skill for protecting and growing your wealth. The world is constantly evolving, and economic, technological, and social conditions can shift in unexpected ways. What works today may not be relevant tomorrow, and understanding this reality helps you maintain a flexible mindset and be prepared to face the unexpected. Adapting doesn't mean reacting without thinking; it means observing, analyzing, and adjusting your strategy to remain successful no matter the circumstances.

A key aspect of adapting to change is accepting that uncertainty will always be present. No one can accurately predict what will happen in the future, but you can prepare for different scenarios. This involves diversifying your investments, keeping an eye on market trends, and maintaining a constant stream of learning. For example, if a new technology is transforming an industry you have financial interests in, it's important to research how it might affect you and consider whether you need to change your strategy. Adaptation starts with information, and staying informed is your best defense against the unexpected.

Flexibility in your decisions is another important element. Often, emotional attachment to certain businesses, investments, or ideas can hinder your ability to adapt. Maybe you have a company that you have run for years or an investment that has always been profitable, but if circumstances change and those options are no longer viable, holding on to them can be detrimental. Learning to let go when necessary and redirect your resources toward more promising opportunities is essential to protecting your fortune. The key is to be pragmatic and evaluate each situation from a rational, not an emotional, point of view.

A common example of change that many face is technological advancement. Technology can be both a threat and an opportunity, depending on how you approach it. On one hand, it can make certain businesses or industries obsolete; on the other, it can open doors to new ways of generating wealth. If you keep an open mind and are willing to learn, you can leverage technology to improve your operations, automate processes, or even explore new investments. Adapting to technological advancements not only keeps you competitive, but it also positions you to take advantage of the opportunities that arise with each innovation.

The global economy is also an area where changes are inevitable. Recessions, changes in government policies, and market fluctuations can affect even the most solid fortunes. To adapt to these changes, it's important to take a proactive rather than reactive approach. This means building a solid emergency fund, maintaining efficient tax planning, and being prepared to adjust your investments as needed. While you can't control the direction of the economy, you can control how you prepare to navigate its ups and downs.

Another aspect of adapting to change is recognizing that you don't need to do it alone. Surround yourself with experts and advisors who can help you interpret the changes and make informed decisions. This can include financial consultants, wealth attorneys, or even mentors with experience in key industries. Having a support network gives you access to perspectives and knowledge that can be crucial in times of uncertainty. However, remember that while experts can guide you, the ultimate responsibility for protecting your wealth always lies with you.

Furthermore, not all changes are external. Throughout your life, your own goals, priorities, and values may evolve. Perhaps in the past you were focused on maximizing your income, but now you prefer to invest in social causes or the well-being of your family. Adapting also means re-evaluating your personal goals and making sure your financial strategy is aligned with them. This process of self-evaluation helps you maintain a healthy relationship with your wealth and ensure that you are using your resources in a way that truly satisfies you.

Communication also plays a crucial role in adaptation. If you have a family or team that depends on you, it's important to keep them informed and engaged with any necessary changes. Transparency builds trust and ensures that everyone is working toward the same goals. For example, if you decide to change the family investment strategy, explaining the reasons behind that decision helps reduce resistance and gain their support. Adapting to changes is easier when you have the support of the key people in your life.

Finally, adapting to change requires a growth mindset. Instead of fearing the unknown, view every change as an opportunity to learn and evolve. Resilience is not the absence of challenges, but the ability to face them with confidence and determination. Every change you face gives you the opportunity to improve your skills, strengthen your strategy, and grow as a person. Instead of resisting change, embrace it as a natural part of life and wealth management.

Adapting to change not only protects your wealth, but also allows you to fully enjoy it. Knowing that you can face any challenge with confidence and preparation gives you peace of mind and freedom. In the end, the ability to adapt is not just a financial skill, but a tool to live a more fulfilling and resilient life. Changes are inevitable, but how you deal with them defines not only your financial success, but also your personal legacy.

The Dangers of the Millionaire Lifestyle

The millionaire lifestyle has an almost mythical appeal. Luxury cars, impressive mansions, exotic travel, and seemingly total freedom are the images that often come to mind when we think of the life of someone with great wealth. However, behind this dazzling facade are real dangers that can affect not only your wealth, but also your emotional well-being, your relationships, and your sense of purpose. Knowing these risks and addressing them consciously is crucial to protecting both your fortune and your happiness.

One of the most common dangers is uncontrolled spending. When you have access to unlimited resources, it's easy to fall into the temptation of mindless spending. Buying a sports car or an expensive piece of jewelry may seem like a small decision when your bank account is robust, but the habit of impulsive spending can quickly add up. The problem isn't the spending itself, but the lack of planning. If you don't set clear limits and financial priorities, you can find yourself in a spending spiral that, in the long run, negatively affects your wealth.

Another risk is the social circle you may attract with your wealth. Having money often attracts people interested in taking advantage of your success. They may present themselves as friends, business partners, or even distant relatives, but their true interest may be in profiting from your fortune. These relationships can be damaging not only financially, but also emotionally. To protect yourself, it's important to be selective about the people you allow into your life and evaluate their intentions. Surround yourself with those who value you for who you are, not what you have.

The millionaire lifestyle can also lead to a disconnect with reality. When you can afford anything, it's easy to lose your sense of the value of money and the effort required to earn it. This can make you insensitive to the challenges faced by people with fewer resources, and in the long run, it can erode your empathy. Staying connected to activities and communities outside of your wealth bubble is one way to combat this problem. Participating in philanthropic activities, collaborating with community organizations, or simply maintaining authentic relationships with people from different backgrounds can help keep you grounded.

Additionally, the pressure to maintain a high lifestyle can be overwhelming. Once you get used to certain standards, it can be difficult to back away, even if circumstances require it. For example, if your income drops or you face an economic crisis, cutting back on expenses can feel like a failure rather than a logical decision. This type of pressure can lead you to make unwise financial decisions, such as taking on unnecessary debt to keep up appearances. The solution is to remember that your worth is not defined by what you own and that flexibility is key to good financial management.

Emotional health can also be affected by the millionaire lifestyle. Wealth can amplify pre-existing issues such as anxiety, stress, or even depression. In some cases, a constant fear of losing what you have can arise, leading to a sense of insecurity despite your success. You may also feel isolated, especially if you perceive that people around you do not understand your concerns or see you solely as a source of resources. Seeking professional support, such as a therapist or coach, can be a valuable tool in managing these challenges.

Another significant danger is the negative influence that the millionaire lifestyle can have on your family, especially your children. When children grow up surrounded by limitless abundance, they can develop a lack of appreciation for effort and the value of work. They may also struggle to find their identity, as the shadow of family wealth can be overwhelming. The solution is to educate them in solid principles of financial responsibility and human values. Teaching them to appreciate effort and manage resources will give them tools to face the world in a balanced way.

Fraud and scams are another constant risk for people with great wealth. The exposure that comes with the millionaire lifestyle can make you a target for sophisticated scammers. From fraudulent investment proposals to complex schemes designed to take advantage of your trust, the risks are myriad. The best defense is diligence. Never make important decisions without doing thorough research and consulting experts you trust. A good team of financial and legal advisors can help you identify and avoid threats before they become problems.

Finally, there is the danger of losing purpose. Wealth can provide you with freedom, but it can also take away your sense of direction if you are not clear about what really matters to you. Many people fall into the trap of chasing more money, thinking this will bring them more happiness, only to find that the emptiness persists. Finding activities and goals that you are passionate about, beyond accumulating material goods, is essential to maintaining a healthy balance. This could be building a legacy, contributing to meaningful causes, or simply enjoying time with loved ones.

The millionaire lifestyle, while full of advantages, is not without its challenges. The dangers can be subtle and often develop over time, but if you are aware of them and take steps to mitigate them, you can enjoy your wealth without compromising your happiness or well-being. Remember that wealth is a tool, not an end in itself, and it is up to you to use it in ways that enrich your life and the lives of those around you.

Identifying Threats and Risks

Identifying threats and risks is an essential skill for anyone who has achieved a significant level of financial success. Having a large fortune not only opens doors to opportunities, but also exposes you to a series of dangers that, if not managed correctly, can compromise your wealth, your peace of mind and even your legacy. This chapter aims to help you understand how to identify these threats and how to protect yourself from them, using clear and effective strategies.

The first step in identifying risks is to accept that no one, no matter how prepared, is completely safe. The idea that a big bank account is a shield against all trouble is an illusion. Risks can come from many directions: ill-informed financial decisions, scams, economic fluctuations, changes in tax laws, family problems, and more. Ignoring these possibilities only leaves you vulnerable. Instead of viewing risks as a negative, see them as an opportunity to be proactive and protect what you've worked so hard to build.

One of the most common and underestimated threats is a lack of diversification in your investments. If you put most of your money in a single type of asset, such as real estate or shares in a single company, you are exposing your fortune to significant risks. For example, if the industry you have invested in experiences a crisis, you can lose a considerable part of your wealth. Diversifying not only across sectors, but also geographically, considerably reduces this risk. The key is to constantly analyze your portfolio and adjust it to balance opportunities with potential dangers.

Another major risk comes from overexposure. Many successful people become public figures, either by choice or because of media interest. This visibility can attract unwanted attention from people with malicious intent, such as scammers, opportunists, and even potential litigants who see your wealth as an opportunity to take advantage. This is where discretion becomes a vital tool. You don't need to hide, but you do need to be mindful of what information you share and with whom.

The legal and tax environment can also pose a significant threat. Laws and regulations are constantly changing, and what seems like a solid financial structure today can become vulnerable due to changes in your country's tax or legal policies. Maintaining a team of specialized lawyers and accountants who are always up to date is essential to anticipate these changes and minimize their impact. It's not just about complying with the law, but understanding it and using it to your advantage.

Emotional and personal risks should not be underestimated. One of the biggest threats to any wealthy person is the mismanagement of emotions, such as overconfidence, fear, or even greed. These emotions can lead you to make rash decisions, such as impulsive investments, risky business ventures, or unnecessary spending. Recognizing when your emotions are influencing your financial decisions is an important step toward staying in control. Talking to a mentor or advisor during times of uncertainty can help you make more objective decisions.

Family relationships can also be an area fraught with risk. Disagreements over the distribution of wealth, the management of family businesses, or even expectations of financial support can lead to serious tensions. The key to minimizing these risks is open and transparent communication. Establishing a clear plan for inheritance and management of family assets, preferably with the help of a mediator or advisor, can prevent conflicts before they arise. In addition, it is important that each family member understands his or her role and responsibilities within the management of the estate.

Fraud is another constant threat. As your wealth grows, so does the likelihood that you will become a target for scammers. These can come in the form of too-good-to-be-true investments, dubious business offers, or even internal fraud within your own organization. The best defense against this is due diligence. Before you commit to any project or investment, conduct thorough research and consult with experts. Additionally, implementing regular audits on your companies and personal assets can help you spot problems before they become serious.

Finally, global crises, such as pandemics, wars, or economic downturns, are threats that no one can accurately predict, but which can have a devastating impact. These situations highlight the importance of having an emergency fund and contingency strategies. This includes having liquid assets, diversifying your investments in international markets, and maintaining open lines of communication with your financial advisors to adjust your strategy quickly if circumstances require it.

Identifying threats and risks doesn't mean living in fear, but rather in preparation. Every risk you face has a solution or a way to mitigate it, as long as you recognize it in time. With a clear vision, the right support, and a constant willingness to learn and adapt, you can effectively protect your fortune. Your wealth should not be a source of worry, but rather a tool that allows you to live fully and build a lasting legacy. The key is to always be alert and make informed decisions to face any challenge that comes your way.

Taking Care of your Emotional and Financial Well-Being

Taking care of your emotional and financial well-being is essential to fully enjoying your success and maintaining balance in your life. Having money does not guarantee happiness or peace of mind if you are not emotionally at peace and do not manage your finances in a healthy way. This chapter aims to help you understand the relationship between your emotions and your money, and how to strengthen both areas to live a more balanced and fulfilling life.

Emotional and financial well-being are more connected than many people think. Money can be a source of stress if not managed properly. For example, the fear of losing it, the weight of responsibilities that come with it, or the expectations of others can create a significant emotional burden. On the other hand, an unstable emotional state can lead you to make impulsive financial decisions, such as excessive spending or poorly calculated investments. Therefore, taking care of both areas simultaneously is key to maintaining a harmonious life.

The first step in taking care of your emotional well-being is to recognize how you feel about your wealth. Many people who reach a high financial level experience emotions such as guilt, fear, or anxiety. Guilt can arise if you feel like you have more than you need while others are struggling to survive. Fear can arise at the possibility of losing what you have earned. Anxiety can creep in when you try to meet the expectations of others or maintain a lifestyle that seems obligatory. Recognizing these emotions is the first step to managing them.

It's critical to set clear boundaries on how and how much of your wealth you allow to affect your personal life. You don't need to say yes to every request for financial help or commit to projects that don't resonate with you just because you feel obligated. Learn to say no in a respectful but firm way. This not only protects your money, but also your emotional health. Remember that your time and energy are resources just as valuable as your money, and they should be used wisely.

Another way to take care of your emotional well-being is to find a deeper purpose for your wealth. Money alone doesn't give meaning to life. Reflect on how you can use your fortune to improve your life and the lives of those around you in a way that makes you feel fulfilled. This can include supporting causes you are passionate about, investing in projects that have a positive impact, or simply creating meaningful experiences for yourself and your loved ones. When your money is aligned with your values, it becomes a source of satisfaction rather than stress.

When it comes to financial well-being, the key is to develop healthy, sustainable habits. This starts with a clear, well-structured financial plan. Even if you already have wealth, it's important to allocate a budget that allows you to enjoy your money without putting your wealth at risk. Set categories for your spending, savings, and investments, and be sure to review your plan regularly to adjust as needed. A solid financial plan not only protects your money, but it also reduces the uncertainty and anxiety associated with managing it.

Additionally, continuing financial education is essential. The world of finance is constantly changing, and what worked ten years ago may not be relevant today. Learn about new trends, technologies, and strategies that can help you maintain and grow your wealth. Consult with experts in the field and don't be afraid to ask questions or seek professional advice. Being well-informed gives you greater confidence in your decisions and reduces the stress associated with managing your wealth.

It's also important to establish a work-life balance. Many wealthy people fall into the trap of constantly working to maintain their wealth, neglecting their emotional health and personal relationships. Make time for activities you enjoy, spend time with loved ones, and prioritize your physical well-being. A balanced life is not only more fulfilling, but it also allows you to make better financial decisions since you're not acting from a place of exhaustion or stress.

Finally, seek emotional support when you need it. Talking to a therapist, life coach, or even a trusted friend can help you process your emotions and deal with the challenges of managing great wealth. Having someone to share your worries and triumphs with can ease the emotional burden and give you a clearer perspective.

Emotional and financial well-being are not achieved overnight. It is an ongoing process that requires attention and care. However, investing in both areas will allow you to enjoy the fruits of your labor in a more fulfilling and satisfying way. Remember that wealth is not just a number in your bank account, but a tool to build a life that is truly worth living. By taking care of your emotions and your money, you are taking care of yourself and ensuring that your success is truly complete.